*Presented to*

_____

*On the occasion of*

_____

*From*

_____

*Date*

_____

# CHARLES COLSON

## *The* Enduring Revolution

*The Battle to Change the Human Heart*

Published by  Barbour & Company, Inc.
              P.O. Box 719
              Uhrichsville, Ohio  44683
              e-mail: books<barbour@tusco.net>

 Member of the
Evangelical Christian
Publishers Association

Printed in the United States of America.

## Introduction

On September 2, 1993, Charles Colson delivered the Templeton Address at the University of Chicago. Such an address is customary following the receipt of the Templeton Prize for Progress in Religion, which had been awarded to Colson earlier in the year. But what was surprising was the nature of his remarks.

In the audience on that auspicious day were men and women of various faiths, many of whom were delegates of the Parliament of the World's Religions. To them—and to us—Colson boldly avers that the only hope for the future of the world and western civilization is the Christian conversion of the human heart. This is "The Enduring Revolution."

Only by claiming our Judeo-Christian heritage can nations of the West hope, once again, to inspire public and personal virtue and give "divine mercy a human face." Only when

5

every human soul is on "a path of immortality" will every man and woman "be treated as the child of a King."

The course of such a revolution will be fraught with discouragement, but as Christians, we have "neither the reason nor the right" to give up the fight. Charles Colson challenges the faithful to remember the sacrifice of the Cross, to rejoice in the Resurrection, and to reap the rewards of a Christian culture: humility, service, and peace.

"LIBERTY IS THE HIGHEST POLITICAL END OF MAN . . . [BUT] NO COUNTRY CAN BE FREE WITHOUT RELIGION."

LORD ACTON

# I SPEAK

as one transformed by Jesus Christ, the living God. He is the Way, the Truth, and the Life. He has lived in me for 20 years. His presence is the sole explanation for whatever is praiseworthy in my work, the only reason for my receiving this award (the Templeton Prize).

That is more than a statement about myself. It is a claim to truth. It is a claim that may contradict your own.

Yet on this, at least, we must agree: the right to do what I've just done—to state my faith without fear—is the first human right. Religious liberty is the essence of human dignity. We cannot build our temples on the ruins of individual conscience. For faith does not come through the weight of power, but through the hope of glory.

It is a sad fact that religious oppression is often practiced by religious groups. Sad—and inexcusable. A believer may risk prison for his own religious beliefs, but he may never build prisons for those of other beliefs.

It is our obligation—all of us here—to bring back a renewed passion for religious liberty to every nation from which we came. It is our duty to create a cultural environment where conscience can flourish. I say this for the sake of every believer imprisoned for boldness or silenced by fear. I say this for the sake of every society that has yet to learn the benefits of vital and voluntary religious faith.

The beliefs that divide us should not be minimized. But neither should the aspirations we share: for spiritual understanding; for justice and compassion; for stewardship of God's creation; for religious influence—not oppression—in the right ordering of society. And for truth against the arrogant lies of our modern age.

For at the close of this century, every religious tradition finds common ground in a common task—a struggle over the meaning and future of our world and our own particular culture. Each of us has an obligation to expose the deceptions that are incompatible with true faith.

A BELIEVER MAY RISK
PRISON FOR HIS OWN
RELIGIOUS BELIEFS,
BUT HE MAY NEVER
BUILD PRISONS
FOR THOSE
OF OTHER BELIEFS.

# THE FOUR HORSEMEN

**FOUR** great myths define our times—the four horsemen of the present apocalypse.

The first myth is the **goodness of man.** The first horseman rails against heaven with the presumptuous question: Why do bad things happen to good people? He multiplies evil by denying its existence.

This myth deludes people into thinking that they are always victims, never villains; always deprived, never depraved. It dismisses responsibility as the teaching of a darker age. It can excuse any crime, because it can always blame something else—a sickness of society or a sickness of the mind.

One writer called the modern age "the golden age of exoneration." When guilt is dismissed as the illusion of narrow minds, then no one is accountable, even to his conscience.

14

The irony is that this should come alive in this century, of all centuries, with its gulags and death camps and killing fields. As G.K. Chesterton once said, the doctrine of original sin is the only philosophy empirically validated by the centuries of recorded human history.

It was a holocaust survivor who exposed this myth most eloquently. Yehiel Dinur was a witness during the trial of Adolf Eichmann. Dinur entered the courtroom and stared at the man behind the bulletproof glass—the man who had presided over the slaughter of millions. The court was hushed as a victim confronted a butcher.

Then suddenly Dinur began to sob, and collapsed to the floor. Not out of anger or bitterness. As he explained later in an interview, what struck him at that instant was a terrifying realization. "I was afraid about myself," Dinur said. "I saw that I am capable to do this... Exactly like he."

The reporter interviewing Dinur understood precisely. "How was it possible for a man to act as Eichmann acted?" he asked. "Was he a monster? A madman? Or was he perhaps something even more terrifying...Was he normal?"

Yehiel Dinur, in a moment of chilling clarity, saw the skull beneath the skin. "Eichmann," he concluded, "is in all of us."

Jesus said it plainly: "That which proceeds out of the man, that is what defiles the man" (Mark 7:20).

The second myth of modernity is the promise of **coming utopia.** The second horseman arrives with sword and slaughter.

This is the myth that human nature can be perfected by government; that a new Jerusalem can be built using the tools of politics.

From the birth of this century, ruthless ideologies claimed history as their own. They moved from nation to nation on the strength of a promised utopia. They pledged to move the world, but could only stain it with blood.

In communism and fascism we have seen rulers who bear the mark of Cain as a badge of honor; who pursue a savage virtue, devoid of humility and humanity. We have seen more people killed in this century by their own governments than in all its wars combined. We have seen every utopian experiment fall exhausted from the pace of its own brutality.

Yet utopian temptations persist, even in the world's democracies—stripped of their terrors perhaps, but not of their risks. The political illusion still deceives, whether it is called the great society, the new covenant, or the new world order. In each case it promises government solutions to our deepest needs for security, peace, and meaning.

The third myth is the **relativity of moral values.** The third horseman sows chaos and confusion.

This myth hides the dividing line between good and evil, noble and base. It has thus created a crisis in the realm of truth. When a society abandons its transcendent values, each individual's moral vision be-comes purely personal and finally equal. Society be-comes merely the sum total of individual preferences, and since no preference is morally preferable, anything that can be dared will be permitted.

This leaves the moral consensus for our laws and manners in tatters. Moral neutrality slips into moral relativism. Tolerance substitutes for truth, indifference for religious conviction. And in the end, confusion undercuts all our creeds.

The fourth modern myth is **radical individualism.** The fourth horseman brings excess and isolation.

This myth dismisses the importance of family, church, and community; denies the value of sacrifice; and elevates individual rights and pleasures as the ultimate social value.

But with no higher principles to live by, men and women suffocate under their own expanding pleasures. Consumerism becomes empty and leveling, leaving society full of possessions but drained of ideals. This is what Vaclav Havel calls "totalitarian consumerism."

A psychologist tells the story of a despairing young woman, spent in an endless round of parties, exhausted by the pursuit of pleasure. When told she should simply stop, she responded, "You mean I don't have to do what I want to do?"

As author George MacDonald once wrote, "The one principle of hell is 'I am my own.'"

WHEN GUILT
IS DISMISSED
AS THE ILLUSION
OF NARROW MINDS,
THEN NO ONE
IS ACCOUNTABLE,
EVEN TO HIS
CONSCIENCE.

# MODERNITY:
## a
# CASE STUDY

# I HAVE

seen firsthand the kind of society these deadly myths create. In 17 years I have been in more prisons that I can count, in more nations than I can name. I have seen the face of the crisis of modernity in real human faces.

The myth of human goodness tells men and women they are not responsible for their action, that everyone is a victim. "Poverty is the cause of crime," said a U.S. attorney general three decades ago. "Looters are not to blame for looting," said a U.S. president. Thus excused, millions refused accountability for their behavior; crime soared—and is today the great plague on civilized societies.

Utopianism, however, assures us that crime can be solved by government policy. On the left, that means rehabilitation; on the right, more and tougher laws to scare people straight. But, our efforts prove futile. In the past 30 years, the prison population in America has increased five-fold. But violent crime has increased just as fast.

For criminals are not made by sociological or environmental or economic forces. They are created by their own moral choices. Institutions of cold steel and bars are unable to reach the human heart, and so they can neither deter nor rehabilitate.

A decade ago, social scientist James Q. Wilson searched for some correlation between crime and social forces. He discovered that in the late nineteenth century, when the nation was rapidly industrializing—conditions that should have caused crime to increase—crime actually declined. The explanation? At the time a powerful spiritual awakening was sweeping across America, inspiring moral revival and social renewal. By contrast, in the affluent 1920s, when there should have been less economic incentive for lawlessness, crime increased. Why? In the wake of Freud and Darwin, religion fell from favor. In Wilson's words, "The educated classes began to repudiate moral uplift."

A similar study in England by Professor Christie Davies found that crime was lowest a century ago when three out of four young Britons were enrolled in Sunday school. Since then, Sunday school attendance has declined, and crime has correspondingly increased.

Crime is a mirror of a community's moral state. A society cannot long survive if the demands of human dignity are not written on our hearts. No number of police can enforce order; no threat of punishment can create it. Crime and violence frustrate every political answer, because there can be no solution apart from character and creed.

But relativism and individualism have

undermined the traditional beliefs that once informed our character and defined our creed. There are no standards to guide us. Dostoyevsky's diagnosis was correct: Without God, everything is permissible; crime is inevitable.

These myths constitute a threat for all of us, regardless of our culture or the faith communities we represent. The four horsemen of the present apocalypse lead away from the cloud and fire of God's presence into a barren wilderness. Modernity was once judged by the heights of its aspirations. Today it must be judged by the depth of its decadence. That decadence has marked the West most deeply; this makes it imperative that we understand the struggle for the soul of western civilization.

CRIME AND VIOLENCE
FRUSTRATE
EVERY POLITICAL ANSWER,
BECAUSE THERE CAN BE
NO SOLUTION
APART FROM
CHARACTER AND CREED.

# The Paradox of Our Times

**WE** stand at a pivotal moment in history, when nations around the world are looking westward. In the past five years, the balance of world power shifted dramatically. Suddenly, remarkably, almost inexplicably, one of history's most sustained assaults on freedom collapsed before our eyes.

The world has been changed, not through the militant dialectic of communism, but through the power of unarmed truth. It found revolution in the highest hopes of common men. Love of liberty steeled under the weight of tyranny; the path of the future was charted in prison cells.

This revolution's symbolic moment was May Day 1990. Protesters followed the tanks, missiles, and troops rumbling across Red Square. One, a bearded Orthodox monk, darted under the reviewing stand where Gorbachev and other Soviet leaders stood. He thrust a huge crucifix into the air, shouting above the crowd, "Mikhail Sergeyevich! Christ is risen!"

Gorbachev turned and walked off the platform.

Across a continent the signal went. In defiant hope a spell was broken. The lies of decades were exposed. Fear and terror fled. And millions awoke as from a long nightmare.

Their waking dream is a world revolution. Almost overnight the western model of economic, political, and social liberty has captured the imagination of reformers and given hope to the oppressed. We saw it at Tiananmen Square, where a replica of the Statue of Liberty, an icon of western freedom, became a symbol of Chinese hope. We saw it in Czechoslovakia when a worker stood before a desolate factory and read to a crowd, with tears in his eyes, the American Declaration of Independence.

This is one of history's defining moments. The faults of the West are evident—but equally evident are the extraordinary gifts it has to offer the world. The gift of markets that increase living standards and choices. The gift of political institutions where power flows from the consent of the governed, not the barrel of a gun. The gift of social beliefs that encourage tolerance and individual autonomy.

Free markets. Free governments. Free minds.

But just at this moment, after the struggle of this century . . . just at this moment, with a new era of liberty our realistic hope . . . just at this moment, the culture that fashioned this freedom is being overrun by the four horsemen. It has embraced the destructive myths of modernity, which are poisoning its wellspring of justice, virtue, and stripping away its most essential humanizing, civilizing influence.

THE WORLD...FOUND
REVOLUTION
IN THE HIGHEST HOPES
OF COMMON MEN.

# Roots

## OF THE
## Western Ideal

# MAKE

no mistake: This humanizing, civilizing influence is the Judeo-Christian heritage. It is a heritage brought to life anew in each generation by men and women whose lives are transformed by the living God and filled with holy conviction.

Despite the failures of some of its followers—the crusades and inquisitions—this heritage has laid the foundations of freedom in the West. It has established a standard of justice over both men and nations. It has proclaimed a higher law that exposes the pretensions of tyrants. It has taught that every human soul is on a path of immortality, that every man and woman is to be treated as the child of a King.

This muscular faith has motivated excellence in art and discovery in science. It has undergirded an ethic of work and an ethic of service. It has tempered freedom with internal restraint, so our laws could be permissive while our society was not.

Christian conviction inspires public virtue, the moral impulse to *do* good. It has sent legions into battle against disease, oppression, and bigotry. It ended the slave trade, built hospitals and orphanages, tamed the brutality of mental wards and prisons.

In every age it has given divine mercy a human face in the lives of those who follow Christ—from Francis of Assisi to the great social reformers Wilberforce and Shaftesbury to Mother Teresa to the tens of thousands of Prison Fellowship volunteers who take hope to the captives—and who are the true recipients of this award.

Christian conviction also shapes personal virtue, the moral imperative to be good. It subdues an obstinate will. It ties a tether to self-interest and violence.

35

Finally, Christian conviction provides a principled belief in human freedom. As Lord Acton explained, "Liberty is the highest political end of man . . . [But] no country can be free without religion. It creates and strengthens the notion of duty. If men are not kept straight by duty, they must be by fear. The more they are kept by fear, the less they are free. The greater the strength of duty, the greater the liberty."

The kind of duty to which Acton refers is driven by the most compelling motivation. I and every other Christian have experienced it. It is the duty that flows from gratitude to God that He would send His only Son to die so we might live.

"IF MEN ARE NOT KEPT
STRAIGHT BY DUTY,
THEY MUST BE BY FEAR.
THE MORE THEY ARE KEPT
BY FEAR,
THE LESS THEY ARE FREE."

LORD ACTON

"THE GREATER
THE STRENGTH OF DUTY,
THE GREATER
THE LIBERTY."

LORD ACTON

# THE FOUR HORSEMEN IN THE WEST

**THIS** is the lesson of centuries: that ordered liberty is one of faith's triumphs. And yet, western cultural and political elites seem blinded by modernity's myths to the historic civilizing role of Christian faith. And so, in the guise of pluralism and tolerance, they have set about to exile religion from our common life. They use the power of the media and the law like steel wool to scrub public debates and public places bare of religious ideas and symbols. But what is left is sterile and featureless and cold.

These elites seek freedom without self-restraint, liberty without standards. But they find instead the revenge of offended absolutes.

Courts strike down even perfunctory prayers, and we are surprised that schools, bristling with barbed wire, look more like prisons than prisons do.

Universities reject the very idea of truth, and we are shocked when the best and the brightest of their graduates loot and betray.

Celebrities mock the traditional family, even revile it as a form of slavery, and we are appalled at the human tragedy of broken homes and millions of unwed mothers.

The media celebrate sex without responsibility, and we are horrified by sexual plagues.

Our lawmakers justify the taking of innocent life in sterile clinics, and we are terrorized by the disregard for life in blood-soaked streets.

C. S. Lewis described this irony a generation ago. "We laugh at honor," he said, "and are shocked to find traitors in our midst...We castrate and bid the geldings be fruitful."

A generation of cultural leaders wants to live off the spiritual capital of its inheritance, while denigrating the ideals of its ancestors.

It squanders a treasure it no longer values. It celebrates its liberation when it should be trembling for its future.

THIS IS THE LESSON
OF CENTURIES:
THAT ORDERED LIBERTY
IS ONE OF FAITH'S
TRIUMPHS.

A GENERATION
OF CULTURAL LEADERS...
CELEBRATES
ITS LIBERATION
WHEN IT SHOULD BE
TREMBLING
FOR ITS FUTURE.

# THE PATH TO TYRANNY

WHERE does the stampede of the four horsemen lead us? Only one place: tyranny. A new kind of cultural tyranny that finds minds, uninformed by traditions and standards, easy to shape.

Philosopher Hannah Arendt described totalitarianism as a process where lonely, rootless individuals, deprived of meaning and community, welcome the captivity of ideology. To escape their inner emptiness, they seek out new forms of servitude. Trading independence for security, they blend into faceless conformity.

The lonely crowd always finds a leader. It submits to the party line and calls it freedom. America is filled with willing recruits to follow a new Grand Inquisitor.

This coming cultural tyranny already casts its shadow across university campuses where repressive speech codes stifle free debate; across courthouses and legislatures where officials hunt down and purge every religious symbol; across network news-rooms and board rooms where nothing is censored except traditional belief. Our modern elites speak of enlightened tolerance while preparing shackles for those who disagree. This is what Chesterton defined as true bigotry: "the anger of men who have no convictions."

Disdaining the past and its values, we flee the judgment of the dead. We tear down memory's monuments—removing every guidepost and landmark—and wander in unfamiliar country. But it is a sterile wasteland in which men and women are left with carefully furnished lives and utterly barren souls.

And so, paradoxically, at the very moment much of the rest of the world seems to be reaching out for western liberal ideas, the West itself, beguiled by myths of modernity, is undermining the very foundation of those ideals.

This is irony without humor—farce without joy. Western elites are carefully separating the wheat from the chaff and keeping the chaff. They are performing a modern miracle of turning wine into water.

This crisis is not only alarming, it is also urgent. In earlier times, social patterns were formed over centuries by tradition and intellectual debate, then gradually filtered to the masses. Now, through technology, a social revolution can be wired directly to the brain. It comes through satellites and videos, through pleasing images and catchy tunes. Refugees on a boat from Southern China were recently intercepted by the U. S. Coast Guard: Their entire knowledge of the English language consisted of one acronym, "MTV."

The world's newly developing nations are in a revolution of rising expectations that may become a trap of misplaced hope. Nations that import a western ideal stripped of its soul will find only what we have found: pleasures as shallow as the moment, emptiness as deep as eternity.

NATIONS THAT IMPORT
A WESTERN IDEAL
STRIPPED OF ITS SOUL
WILL FIND ONLY
WHAT WE HAVE FOUND:
PLEASURES AS SHALLOW
AS THE MOMENT,
EMPTINESS AS DEEP
AS ETERNITY.

# THE
# CONTEMPORARY
# CHALLENGE

# I SAY

to you assembled here today from every part of the globe that this is a challenge facing all of us. At this extraordinary moment in world history, many nations once enslaved to ruthless ideologies have now been set free only to face a momentous decision: Each must decide whether to embrace the myths of modernity or turn to a deeper, older tradition, the half-forgotten teachings of saints and sages.

I say to my compatriots in the West that we bear a particular responsibility—for modernity's myths have found fertile soil in our lands, and we have offered haven to the four horsemen who trample the dreams and hopes of men and women everywhere. As the world looks to us, let us summon the courage to challenge our comfortable assumptions, to scrutinize the effect we have on our global neighbors...and then to recover that which has been the very soul and conscience of our own civilization.

For the West today is like Janus, with a two-sided face—one offering futility, empty secularism and death; the other offering freedom, rich, biblically rooted spirituality, and life. Commentators have described the internal conflict between these two as a culture war. Some have even declared the war over. The four horsemen, they tell us, are the victors at this chapter in our history.

LET US SUMMON
THE COURAGE TO
CHALLENGE OUR
COMFORTABLE
ASSUMPTIONS…
AND THEN TO RECOVER
THAT WHICH HAS BEEN
THE VERY SOUL
AND CONSCIENCE
OF OUR OWN
CIVILIZATION.

# THE
# ENDURING
# REVOLUTION

# ADMITTEDLY the signs are

not auspicious, as I have been at pains to show, and it is easy to become discouraged. But a Christian has neither the reason nor the right. For history's cadence is called with a confident voice. The God of Abraham, Isaac, and Jacob reigns. His plan and purpose rob the future of its fears.

By the Cross He offers hope, by the Resurrection He assures His triumph. This cannot be resisted or delayed. Mankind's only choice is to recognize Him now or in the moment of ultimate judgment. Our only decision is to welcome His rule or to fear it.

But this gives everyone hope. For this is a vision beyond a vain utopia or a timid new world order. It is the vision of an Enduring Revolution. One that breaks more than the chains of tyranny, it breaks the chains of sin and death. And it proclaims a liberation that the cruelest prison cannot contain.

The Templeton Prize is awarded for progress in religion. In a technological age, we often equate progress with breaking through barriers in science and knowledge. But progress does not always mean discovering something new. Sometimes it means rediscovering wisdom that is ancient and eternal. Sometimes, in our search for advancement, we find it only where we began. The greatest progress in religion today is to meet every nation's most urgent need: A revolution that begins in the human heart. It is the Enduring Revolution.

In the aftermath of the tragedy in Waco, Texas, and terrorist bombings in New York, we heard dire warnings, even from the president of the United States, of religious extremism. But that, with due respect, is not the world's gravest threat. Far more dangerous is the decline of true religion and of its humanizing values in our daily lives. No ideology—not even liberal democracy—is sufficient. Every noble hope is empty apart from the Enduring Revolution.

This revolution reaches across centuries and beyond politics. It confounds the ambitions of kings, and rewards the faith of a child. It clothes itself in the rags of common lives, then emerges with sudden splendor. It violates every jaded expectation with the paradox of its power.

The evidence of its power is humility. The evidence of its conquest is peace. The evidence of its triumph is service. But that still, small voice of humility, of peace, of service becomes a thundering judgment that shakes every human institution to its foundation.

The Enduring Revolution teaches that freedom is found in submission to a moral law. It says that duty is our sharpest weapon against fear and tyranny. This revolution raises an unchanging and eternal moral standard—and offers hope to everyone who fails to reach it. This revolution sets the content of justice— and transforms the will to achieve it. It builds communities of character—and of compassion.

On occasion, God provides glimpses of this glory. I witnessed one in an unlikely place: a prison in Brazil like none I've ever seen.

Twenty years ago in the city of San Jose dos Campos, a prison was turned over to two Christian laymen. They called it Humaita, and their plan was to run it on Christian principles.

The prison has only two full-time staff; the rest of the work is done by inmates. Every prisoner is assigned another inmate to whom he is accountable. In addition, every prisoner is assigned a volunteer family from the outside that works with him during his term and after his release. Every prisoner joins a chapel program, or else takes a course in character development.

When I visited Humaita, I found the inmates smiling—particularly the murderer who held the keys, opened the gates, and let me in. Wherever I walked I saw men at peace. I saw clean living areas. I saw people working industriously. The walls were decorated with biblical sayings from Psalms and Proverbs.

Humaita has an astonishing record. Its recidivism rate is 4 percent compared to 75 percent in the rest of Brazil and the United States. How is that possible?

I saw the answer when my inmate guide escorted me to the notorious punishment cell once used for torture. Today, he told me, that block houses only a single inmate. As we reached the end of the long concrete corridor and he put the key into the lock, he paused and asked, "Are you sure you want to go in?"

"Of course," I replied impatiently. "I've

been in isolation cells all over the world."
Slowly he swung open the massive door, and I saw the prisoner in that punishment cell: a crucifix, beautifully carved by the Humaita inmates—the prisoner Jesus, hanging on the cross.

"He's doing time for all the rest of us," my guide said softly.

In that cross carved by loving hands is a holy subversion. It heralds change more radical than mankind's most fevered dreams. Its followers expand the boundaries of a kingdom that can never fail. A shining kingdom that reaches into the darkest corners of every community into the darkest corners of every mind. A kingdom of deathless hope, of restless virtue, of endless peace.

This work proceeds, this hope remains, this fire will not be quenched: The Enduring Revolution of the Cross of Christ.

BY THE CROSS
HE OFFERS HOPE,
BY THE RESURRECTION
HE ASSURES
HIS TRIUMPH.

# About Prison Fellowship

Prison Fellowship is an interdenominational ministry to prisoners, ex-prisoners, and their families, founded in 1976 by Charles W. Colson. After serving seven months in prison for a Watergate-related offense, Colson devoted his life to working with prisoners and their families.

In 1976 he started Prison Fellowship with two staff members and three volunteers. Since that time, Prison Fellowship has grown phenomenally. Some 300 employees and almost 50,000 volunteers work in states across America. Prison Fellowship International has involvement with prison ministry groups in over seventy countries around the world.

Prison Fellowship believes that the first and most important step in true rehabilitation is a spiritual one—when an inmate consciously turns away from the old life to new life in Jesus Christ. But that turning point is only the beginning. Inmates need teaching, guidance, and encouragement, as well as practical life skills. They need role models to help them see how to become respectable citizens who contribute to society. Prison Fellowship has a variety of in-prison and external programs to help accomplish these goals.

If you would like to support our cause or would like to learn more about Prison Fellowship, contact us at the following address:

Prison Fellowship Ministries
P.O. Box 97103
Washington, D.C. 20090-7103
703-478-0100
web site: http://www.pfm.org

**Charles Colson** is chairman of the board of Prison Fellowship, a ministry that exhorts and equips the church to help those suffering at all points in the cycle of crime.  The author of such international bestsellers as *Born Again, Life Sentence, Kingdoms in Conflict,* and *The Body,* Mr. Colson is also a familiar voice with his Christian commentary, "BreakPoint."